P9-CEC-928

Kettle Bottom

Also by Diane Gilliam Fisher

One of Everything, 2003
Recipe for Blackberry Cake, 1999 (chapbook)

Kettle Bottom

■

Diane Gilliam Fisher

PERUGIA PRESS
FLORENCE, MASSACHUSETTS
2004

Copyright © 2004 by Diane Gilliam Fisher

All rights reserved

Perugia Press extends deeply felt thanks to the many individuals whose generosity made the publication of *Kettle Bottom* possible. We recognize in particular The Fund for Women Artists, our fiscal sponsor, for their fundraising service and expertise. For more information about Perugia Press and to make a tax-deductible donation, please contact us directly or visit our Web site.

Book Design by Jeff Potter/Potter Publishing Studio and Susan Kan

Text Composition by Amy Rothstein/Pond Productions

Cover photo is by Marion Post Wolcott (1910–1990). Coal miner's child taking home kerosene for lamps. Company houses, coal tipple in background. Pursglove, Scotts Run, West Virginia, 1938. Library of Congress, Prints & Photographs Division, FSA-OWI Collection, LC-USF33-030180-M2 DLC.

Author photo by Amy Fisher

Library of Congress Cataloging-in-Publication Data

Fisher, Diane Gilliam, 1957-

   Kettle bottom : Diane Gilliam Fisher.

      p. cm.

   Includes bibliographical references.

   ISBN 978-0-9660459-7-0 (alk. paper)

   1. Mingo County (W. Va.)--Poetry.

   2. West Virginia--Poetry. I. Title.

   PS3556.I8132K47 2004

   811'.54--dc22

                   2004002984

Perugia Press

P.O. Box 60364

Florence, MA 01062

info@perugiapress.com

http://www.perugiapress.com

Acknowledgments

Appalachian Heritage: "Violet's Wash"
Appalachian Journal: "Dear Mr. President"
Journal of Kentucky Studies: "What History Means to Me,"
"Out of the Whirlwind"
Pikeville Review: "My Dearest Hazel," "Pink Hollyhocks"
Now & Then: "A Reporter from New York Asks Edith
Mae Chapman, Age Nine, What Her Daddy Tells Her
about the Strike"

Many people read all or part of this manuscript and made suggestions, or otherwise helped it along its way. Special thanks are due to Eleanor Wilner and Ellen Bryant Voigt — tall women in my life who, as the mountain saying goes, cast a long shadow. I also wish to thank Maggie Anderson, David Baker, Jeanne Bryner, Laura Cherry, Patrick Donnelly, Joyce Dyer, Linda Elkin, Richard P. Gabriel, Jannett Highfill, George Ella Lyon, Mary Jane Nealon, Sue Oringel, Sherry Robinson, and Leslie Shinn. As always, I am most grateful for the support and patience of my family, who held the light and waited for me during my long stretches underground.

I am grateful to the Ohio Arts Council for an Individual Artist Fellowship which helped me complete this book.

Contents

Author's Note

The events of the West Virginia mine wars of 1920–1921, grew out of decades of conflict. Subsistence wages, the unwillingness of coal operators to slow production for safety reasons, their intransigence with regard to the rights of the miners to organize — these conditions made enemies of the miners and the operators. The situation was aggravated by the organization of life in the camps, which the companies controlled in every respect. Housing was owned by the company; trade was often limited to company-owned stores; the company brought in the doctor, often built the school and brought in the teacher, built the church and supplied the preacher. Probably the most hated persons employed by the operators were agents of the Baldwin-Felts Detective Agency, out of Bluefield, West Virginia. Commonly referred to by the miners as "gun thugs," the Baldwin-Felts agents were employed to enforce company policies — to spy out union activity, to evict miners connected to the union from company houses, and to provide general, often violent, intimidation throughout the camps.

In May of 1920, Sid Hatfield, police chief of Matewan, in Mingo County, confronted eleven Baldwin-Felts agents sent to turn several families out of their company owned homes. The eviction was thwarted, but the next day a gun battle erupted at the Matewan train depot, leaving dead seven Baldwin-Felts agents, including two brothers of the head of the agency, two miners, and the mayor of Matewan. Following the Matewan Massacre, violence escalated on both sides. Martial law was declared. Baldwin-Felts agents, in a strictly illegal, unconstitutional move, were deputized and allowed to operate in the camps with the full force of the law. When Sid Hatfield was assassinated by

Baldwin-Felts agents on the steps of the McDowell County Courthouse in 1921, the rage of the miners became uncontrollable. Thousands gathered in Logan County to march to "Bloody Mingo County." Federal troops were called in and planes armed with gas were dispatched to put down the miners' revolt. The days of guerilla warfare that ensued are known as the Battle of Blair Mountain. The miners, many of whom were World War I veterans, were convinced to return to their homes, at least partly because they were unwilling to fight against the armed forces they had so recently been part of. Nevertheless, shortly afterwards the UMWA was able to organize the southern West Virginia coal mines. Although negotiations began regarding some of the more hateful conditions in which the miners and their families lived and worked, the events of 1920–1921 did little to better the lives of the miners and their families.

What do you want — a cliff over a city?
A foreland, sloped to sea and overgrown with roses?
These people live here.

— Muriel Rukeyser

I.

Summer ~ Fall

Explosion at Winco No. 9

Delsey Salyer knowed Tom Junior by his toes,
which his steel-toed boots had kept the fire off of.
Betty Rose seen a piece of Willy's ear, the little
notched part where a hound had bit him
when he was a young'un, playing at eating its food.

It is true that it is the men that goes in, but it is us
that carries the mine inside. It is us that listens
to what all they are scared of and takes
the weight of it from them, like handing off
a sack of meal. Us that learns by heart
birthmarks, scars, bends of fingers,
how the teeth set crooked or straight.
Us that picks up the pieces.
                              I didn't have
nothing to patch with but my old blue dress,
and Ted didn't want floweredy goods
on his shirt. I told him, *It's just under your arm,
Ted, it ain't going to show.*
                              They brung out bodies,
you couldn't tell. I seen a piece of my old blue dress
on one of them bodies, blacked with smoke,
but I could tell it was my patch, up under the arm.
When the man writing in the big black book
come around asking about identifying marks,
I said, *blue dress.* I told him, *Maude Stanley, 23.*

L'Inglese

The English is rocky in the mouth,
so many hard sounds they batter the tongue
like coal clattering from the tipple
into the railroad car. It makes a longing
in the ear for a voice to rise and fall
like a fountain. They make new words —
they have no Tasso, they have no Dante
to tell them the names. It is months
I am wondering: What is "kettle bottom,"
il sotto della caldaia, that they fear?
Finally I ask Henry Burgess. He laughs,
he says it is the petrified tree trunk
buried in the mountain, two, three hundred
pounds. *Drops through the mine roof*,
Henry says, and makes a loud clap
with his hands. *Kills a man*
just like that. For such a thing
I would not say "kettle bottom."
For such a thing I would say,
Lasciate ogni speranza
voi ch'entrate qui.

My Dearest Hazel

Momma has wrote me a letter down here
to the camp, telling how you are planning
to marry Turley come fall and how he
has gone in the mine up to Jenkinjoncs
and has took to it like a fish to water. Hazel,
do you remember how Momma used to say
Daddy took to drink like a fish to water?
How she'd make us promise to not never marry
a man that drinks? *Don't pay no mind
to what all he says, girls,* she'd say,
you smell it on his breath, you walk away.
Drinking ain't the only thing, Hazel.
Some men, they get in the mine, and it gets them.
They won't do nothing else, nor care
anymore for what goes on in the sun. My Clayton,
his lungs is so full of dust, some nights
he can't hardly draw breath. But he won't
go back to farming, even though Momma'd give us
a stake on the home place. If Turley
is taking to it like that, Hazel, walk away.
I'm telling you, Hazel, for the sake of your own
sweet soul, when Clayton kisses me now
I don't taste nothing but coal.

The Rocks Down Here

First hour of every shift down in the mine,
shakes and cold sweats worse'n the grippe
that near took me last spring.
Past that, I begin to feel easy-like,
moving through the dark.
You can bet your bottom dollar
them Baldwin-Felts gun thugs
won't hound a man down into the hole
to devil him. Nor can a woman's eyes
follow after him, craving
to be somewhere else, somewhere clean
in green leaves and sun, where she don't
spend her days wiping coal dust
and scraping to feed young'uns. Seven
is hard to feed. The rocks down here,
they don't expect nobody to love them
and they don't never need shoes, nor get
all big-eyed and hungry, looking
at a man. After an hour or so
down below, a body gets to thinking,
a mountain on your back, hell,
that ain't nothing.

Dear Diary

My teacher, Miss Terry, has give me this little book,
for a girl, she says, has got lots of feelings
she needs to get out and maybe she dont want
to tell them to the whole world — that
is what a diary is for. So I will tell you
Dear Diary, all my secrets, beginning
with Emily Lawson.
                  Ever few months,
church ladies in Cincinnati sends us
at Winco a mission box. Mostly it is a big lot
of nothing cant nobody use, but last time
the women begin to Praise Jesus and clap
for it was all coats. They lit into the box
and begin to parcel them out, holding them
up by the shoulder, seeing what fit who.
I just set quiet, but I seen a blue coat in the pile,
so pretty — blue and soft-looking
with a black velvet collar, jet buttons
like little barrels, and shiny black loops.
I didnt say nothing, for it is wrong
to covet, but Granny Chapman, she seen
me looking and she said to Mama,
Well, I do believe that little blue coat
looks made for Edith Mae. I knowed
Mama might frown, for she dont believe
in taking the finest things. The first,
she says, shall be last. Granny Chapman
looked at her hard, though, till Mama smiled
and said, *Why, yes, Edith Mae, come on*
and let us see. All the neighbor women said

Aint she pretty and *Look at them blue eyes*
till I felt like a queen.

When me and Mama went on home and Daddy
seen me in my coat, he commenced
to stomping around, for he is hateful of them
mission boxes, but Mama caught his eye
and shook her head *No* at him.
He just said *Well,* and grunted some
and set back down and looked at me.
Edith Mae, he said finally, *you
are the apple of my eye.*

I run over and clumb up on his lap, which
I have not for a long time, as I am nine,
and hugged his neck and told him, *Daddy,
you are the huckleberry of my heart.*

Later, when Mama and Daddy was abed,
I will tell you, Dear Diary, I snuck
my coat off a the peg, to sleep in. It crackled
under my back from a letter I found, stuck
up under the lining, which says this —

Dear Mountain Girl,

My mother has told me how in the coal camps
of West Virginia there are girls who do not have
dancing lessons or a new coat every year,
or the benefit of scripture or even supper every day.

Mother says I must remember that the last
shall be first, so I have kept last year's coat and send
you the new blue coat Grandmother Lawson
sent me from Boston. I hope it will keep
you warm and make you feel not so poor.

                    Very Truly Yours,
                    Emily Lawson

I dont aim ever to tell, for it is good
when Daddy dont stomp and Mama smiles
and says *Edith Mae, you plenty warm
in that pretty coat?* And I say *Yes, Mama,
warm as pie.* Which is true and not a lie,
for it is only my heart that is cold.

Journal of Catherine Terry
7 September 1920

Like pieces of broken glass tumbling
in a kaleidoscope — so are my thoughts
and nerves and senses constantly jumbled
into patterns which do not hold, which shift
the way millions of green leaves in this place
whisper then retreat, give glimpses
beyond the curtain, then draw closed.
It is like a seasickness to watch them
and to never feel the ground solid.
What sounds in the night like a storm
rising behind the layered horizon of hills
gathers itself into a drone, a drumming
of rain, of heavy fingers, angry,
on a thick wood table, then it groans,
groans, louder, screams — whole nights
punctuated by the lull
and alarm of coal trains.
The darkness here is the dark
of the blind, the dark behind
the blind, the purely unknown.
Wild creatures — they tell me, though
my heart is not resolved to it — shriek
in the night like a chain drawn up
from the center of the earth, weighted
with a cage from Hell, like a woman
dragged up into the woods and
bruted to pieces. Screams, silence,
more screams, it goes on
for an hour or more and no door opens
in the camp, no light goes on — not even mine

for my hand trembled so I could not put
match to wick. I held my wrist
with my left hand to steady it and felt
my pulse, not as a beat, but as
a whirring, so fast did it run, blurred
and wild, racing to get away.

At the Colored Bathhouse

We come on the railroad from Alabama,
me and my brother, not riding
like the dagos, but out in front, timbering
and laying track, we figured, all the way
to Ohio. But the railroad work give out
and we was stuck in Mingo County.
We *colored* here, for some. For some, niggers
and scabs — it twist a face the same
saying both of them names, like wringing out
a dirty dishrag. Like that fire boss sticking
his head in our bathhouse ever shift end —
craning his old chicken neck, whooping up
at our empty pants legs dangling down
from the ceiling on chains — grinning and hollering
String 'em up, boys. That's the way!

Pearlie Asks Her Mama What *Poontang* Means

Mama says to don't tell Daddy, for he
would have to go after them men that spoke
to me that way, and God only knows
what would happen then. But I
would not never want Daddy to know.
And I did not even tell Mama
how the one run up behind me, laughing,
and lifted up the back of my skirt
with a shotgun. Mama says
to don't walk by the store no more, nor go
anywhere at all without her, and I promised.
But I am going to the store one more time.
I have not never stole nothing,
nor hardly ever even told a lie, but I have got
to get me a knife. All my life
I have tried so hard to be so good, and now
it is all for naught, for them men,
them men has put murder in my heart.

Jake and Isom

Stone Mountain Coal come rumbling
through here, rattling money and jobs
in their pockets loud and loose as chunks
of coal in a two-ton car.
I was older, the farm was mine by right.
Jake was seventeen and he figured
he might be done with farming. *Listen,*
I told him, *them people ain't from here.*
No telling how they'll do you. Daddy
left us here, and here we'll stay.
He got him a big eye for them carbide lamps
and them shiny new shovels. Wanted in
with them men with the pockets.
I near begged him, *Don't do it, bud.*
That's a hole a man don't ever get out of.
Dirt's dirt, Isom — he just sassed — *Don't matter*
if you're grubbing up top or digging down below.
You're wrong, Jake, I told him. I said,
There is some kinds of dirt
a man can't wash off.
                          He signed on, they come
up here talking to him like he's a big shot.
Told him we owned the land *ad coelum*
ad infernum — they'd take the hell off our hands
and leave us the heaven. I run them off,
but Jake he snuck down the hill and they drove
him to Naugatuck. Said he was me, and he signed
their paper. Henry Burgess seen them going
into the Courthouse and run hell for leather
back up here — by the time I got to town,
they was gone. Only thing to do, man there said

— which I refused — was to bring the law
down on my brother.
                        I found him back home, sitting
half-scared, half-proud at the kitchen table.
Big bag of soup beans in one hand,
yellow-dog contract in the other.

Violet's Wash

You can't have nothing clean.
I scrubbed like a crazy woman
at Isom's clothes that first week
and here they come off the line, little black
stripes wherever I'd pinned them up
or hung them over — coal dust settles
on the clothesline, piles up
like a line of snow on a tree branch.
After that, I wiped down the clothesline
every time, but no matter, you can't
get it all off. His coveralls is stripy
with black and gray lines,
ankles of his pants is ringed around,
like marks left by shackles.
I thought I'd die that first week
when I seen him walk off to the mine,
black, burnt-looking marks
on his shirt over his shoulders, right
where wings would of folded.

Beautiful, the Owner Says

Yes, it seems unlovely in the daylight.
One winces to see the grime on porch rails
and windowsills, gaunt garments
on clotheslines the only decoration
in the yards, children let to play
in the soot and cinders near the tipple.

But in the dark you see
only what glows.

The coke ovens at night
glow orange, like eyes
opening on the hillside,
like oracles, the founding
of a hearth for a new world.
Carbide lamps winding
their way to the shift house
string together along the road,
serpentine toward the drift mouth
like a Chinese dragon, some ancient
fire-breathing creature guarding
the treasure in the mountain.

Shelva Jean Tells the Sheriff What She Saw

I'd took Woody's dinner bucket to the shift house,
he'd forgot it. Henry Burgess carried it down
on the last trip car. I wasn't even looking
back where they'd unharnessed that pony.
First I seen was that dago boy
waving his arms, hollering something,
who knows what. I wheeled around and seen
a woman in a white dress coming up
behind that pony, carrying a girl-baby,
not no more than two or three year old,
holding her out, under her arms,
fixing to set her on that pony.
Operator's wife, was what I figured.
I could tell by her dress
that woman didn't know nothing.
Them ponies go blind after two,
three months down in the hole, but they know
when something's sneaking up on them.
I didn't have time to open my mouth —
the pony bucked, kicked that baby smack
in the middle of her chest, right out
of her momma's hands. That poor woman
stood there twisting in on herself,
her mouth opening and closing
like she was screaming, but no sound
coming out. Seemed like forever.
Then that dago boy was there. He snatched
that child up and run fit to bust his heart
down the road to the camp, a-wailing
and hollering *doe-tory, doe-tory* all the way.
That is how come him to be covered

with that baby's blood. It is God's truth
and I am aiming to tell it up and down
this holler. They's gonna be hell to pay,
Sheriff, that dago boy turns up dead.

After the Dago Boy Turns Up Dead

I don't know what part Isom done,
but he come home past midnight, bloodied
and puking and caked in mud.
I had figured what was up when I seen him leave,
and I told him then, *Isom, what's done*
is done, y'all can't bring that dago boy back.
I told him, *Now you know your brother*
is like to be up there with them other deputies,
and I don't care if Jake's done turned,
or what he might of done to that dago boy.
He is your blood, Isom. Your blood.
Didn't even turn around. After, he come in
far as the doorway, laid his forehead agin
the doorframe, and begin to cry. Cried
till his legs give out and he set there, elbows
on his knees, sobbing into his hands
till I didn't know what to do or say.
I touched him a little, on the shoulder,
and I said, *Let's get you cleaned up, honey.*
He followed me like a little child
into the back room, just set in the washtub
while I wiped and rinsed. *Get it off, Violet,*
that's all he said. *Get it all off me.* I didn't.
I left a smudge right in the middle
of his forehead, God's mark, so can't
nobody come up here and kill him,
no matter whose blood
cries out from the ground.

A Book Report, by Pearlie Webb

First off, I do not understand what a book report is <u>for</u>. It seems to me books is to <u>read</u>, and it is the author's job to <u>write</u>. Second off, I do not believe being extra smart, as you said I am and that is why I have to write this book report, should mean a person has got to do extra work. But I was not raised in a barn, my mama has taught me *do not sass*, so I will write my book report as I am told.

When you give me this book, Miss Terry, and told me it means *Changes* and these stories helps explain why things is the way they are, I thought, *Well, good. Finally.* For I have asked my mama the why of many things and she has give me the Bible and told me if I look careful and with my heart I will find all the answers there. Well, I find Lot, and I want to know why is Lot a righteous man and the angels wants to save him even after they heared him say to them men on the street — *Take my daughters.* I know what this means, Miss Terry, though I wish I did not, for my mama has told me the what of certain things, even though she cannot tell me the why. So I was glad to get this book. But I am sorry, I do not agree that these *Changes* stories explains a thing. I am hoping you will understand that disagreeing is not the same as sassing and will not mark me down for this. Now, that story about Apollo and Daphne, for example, that might tell you how there come to be that kind of tree, but not how come he can chase her like that, to do her ugly, and <u>she</u> is the one gets turned into a tree. May be you think it is nice to get turned into a laurel, Miss Terry, because they are so perty to look at, but it is not. Their leaves will sick your animals, and if you keep bees, you got to cut out any laurel that's around, for them perty flowers will poison your honey. And when a bunch of them grows all up, that is called a laurel hell, Miss Terry. This is not swearing, this is what you call a geographical <u>term</u>. I do not believe Daphne gets saved in this story, I believe she ends up in a laurel <u>hell</u>.

May be, Miss Terry, my heart is not so good, for I have looked in the Bible as Mama told me, and I have looked in your *Changes* book to find answers, but I do not. It is the <u>same old story</u>, Miss Terry, and I still do not know why.

My Dearest Hazel

I was afeared that was what it was, Hazel,
when I seen you at the wedding, looking
so pale and peaked. Lord help us.
You are right to be scared. It ain't
a time for it. Some folks down here
is already turned out, living in tents
on Al Burgess's place. You know Turley,
Hazel. Your husband ain't one to lay down
and take it, Company starts in to pushing
folks around. You get ready, honey.
Cart all your canned goods
up to Momma's, your quilts,
your pretty dishes — them Baldwin-Felts
breaks things up when they put people out
and you will need to hang on
to whatever you can. As for the other thing
you ask, Hazel, the answer is this:
three tablespoons of sugar and turpentine.

Out of the Whirlwind

Let us call today upon the God
of Job, let us call him down
to Tug River Valley, to the wilderness
that is the black, hard heart of Stone
Mountain Coal. Let him set his face
upon the operators, let him ask,
Hath the rain a father? Out of whose womb
came the ice? and the hoary frost
of heaven, who hath engendered it?
Let us point to the white house on the hill
in answer, and to the frozen tents
down in the valley. Let the God of Job
set down his whirlwind and cry out,
Hast thou given the horse strength?
Hast thou clothed his neck
with thunder? And let the blinded ponies
step forth in answer. Let us step forth
with our wives and our children and say,
We are that food, when Almighty God
demands of the operators of Stone Mountain Coal
Who provideth for the raven his food?

Two Hundred Million Years

1910, STEPP MOUNTAIN

We buried our people up on top of Stepp Mountain,
highest spot on the home place, and the prettiest.
Mama took me up, first time, when I was not no more
than four or five, right after baby Alma died.
Her grave was mounded up and I figured
she was right there in the dirt, but Mama said no,
she was safe in the earth. She said come fall
the rain would soak the mound down even
with the ground. We'd come up every so often,
she said, and we'd see how our hurt
would go down too, like Alma's little mound.

1920, WINCO COAL CAMP

My third-eldest brother, Robert Warren, went in
the mine at sixteen. We'd buried Daddy three days before,
right next to Alma, for even though Daddy had sold
mineral rights to Stone Mountain Coal, he would not
sign till they wrote in the paper how we'd always
have use of the burying ground. The Company
told Mama it was a kettle bottom took Daddy. They say
that a lot — kettle bottom, they figure, ain't nobody's fault.
They give Robert Warren Daddy's tools, and his number,
102. Put him to work in the same room. Roof
sounded hollow, Robert Warren said, but he couldn't see
where no kettle bottom had fell through. He had twelve
days in the hole when his section caved. Company says
couldn't nobody have lived, says they can't go in

for the bodies without risking more men.
Mama says now that whole mountain is a grave.
Two hundred million years, she says,
these here mountains have been around.
We ain't got the life in us, nor the heart
no more, to wait for them to go down.

Ironing

I does it. All the rest, too, I ain't white —
scrub the clothes when they dirty,
feed the children when they hungry, comb
the cinders out of they heads when the train
blast by, spewing like a devil out of the hind end
of Hell. I tend the stove and go to the store
when need be, old goat-bellied storekeeper
cutting his eyes at me ever which way.
I guess ironing be the cleanest
job of work I got. I put it off, though,
and put it off, till it be my most last
work of the day. Since he going in the mine,
Lord, I just hate
dragging out that old cooling board.

The Dancers Are All Gone under the Hill

I never fussed nor primped for the boys,
always went the other way, plain. I wore
cotton washed thin as silk against my young
woman's body — and I never sat out
a dance in my life. Even the knobbiest
boys would gather up their nerve and ask.
Grandma Cobb figured it all for pride,
but what did it hurt me to be kind?
Mostly the boys, they danced like they worked —
not in time to the music, but like the swing
of a hoe, or the turn of the plow at the end
of a furrow. They was hard and thin,
proud with work, shy of their faces.
Grandma Cobb muttered on about *vanity,*
vanity, all is vanity, then there'd be the next one,
holding out his arm, happy, and I bibled her
right back — *A time to dance, Grandma.*
She'd holler, *A time to cast away stones,*
and a time to gather stones together,
like she'd won. Who knew what that meant?
Not me. Not the boys, not even later, I think,
when they went from prying rocks out of the field
to loading coal into two-ton cars.
Not till the rocks started to fall
and the gravel filled their mouths.

Pearlie Tells What Happened at School

Miss Terry has figured since we are living
in a coal camp, we ought to know geology,
which is learning about rocks. Every day
we got to bring in a different rock
and say what it is. Even our spelling words
is rock words, like *sediment* and *petrified*.
Yesterday, Miss Terry says, *Who can use
"petrified" in a sentence?* and Walter Coyle
raises his hand, which, he don't never
say nothing. He's a little touched, Walter is,
ever since his uncle Joe — he was the laughingest,
sparkliest-eyed man you ever seen — ever since Joe
got sealed in at Layland and they ain't never
gonna know if he got burnt up or gassed
or just plain buried. So Walter says,
and he don't never look up from his desk,
he says, *Miss Terry, can a person get petrified?*

Miss Terry thinks he is sassing her, 'cause she
don't know about Joe Coyle, and about
how Walter don't never sleep no more
nor hardly eat enough to keep
a bird alive, as his mama says.
Miss Terry sends him to the cloak room
but Walter, he just walks on out. I reckoned
that was the last we'd see of Walter.
He come back this morning, though, pockets
filled with rocks, and with a poke full of rocks.
Spreads them all out on Miss Terry's desk
'fore she even asks. *Well, alright,* she says,
suppose you tell us what these are.

Walter stirs the rocks around a bit, so gentle,
picks up a flat, roundish one and lays it
agin his cheek. *This here,* he says,
is the hand.

Abe

Much as I love him, I tried
to keep Henry away when all this
union trouble started. I'd tell him,
Honey, now I'm not able for that,
but you can't put a man off
forever. Seemed like I knowed
this would happen. Soon
as I figured it for true, I went
to the granny woman to see
was there any way to get it
to be a girl. She had ways
to tell which it was — you swing
your wedding ring on a string
over your belly, it'll twist
left for a boy, right for a girl.
But child, she said, *what's done
is done. Unless.*
                    No, I told her.
I ain't come for that.

Henry is happy. He wants
Clairy, after his mama,
if it's a girl. I said, quick-like,
*If it's a boy, Abraham,
for Daddy — but call him Abe.*
I don't care for Abraham.
I would not want a name
such as would fool a son
up the mountain to his death.
But I can go with Abe — his secret,
real name will be Abednego.

I want my boy such a name
as talks back to kings and walks
right out of a fiery furnace.

Pink Hollyhocks

I turned the quilt over on the bed
when the neighbor women come in
to cover the mirrors and stop the clocks,
hang black crepe over the doorframe.

Onliest pretty thing I had, that quilt.

Not a old feedsack quilt, but a Wreath
of Hollyhocks, cut from Aunt Zelly's
pattern and done up from a piece
of double-pink Mama brought me
from Kermit, soft Nile green for the leaves,
and new bleached muslin to put it on.
I quilted every inch, stitches no bigger
than a speck of meal. He wasn't home,
night I finished. I put it on the bed,
took my clothes off, and got under it.
When I heard him in the kitchen,
I called and told him it was done,
And you know what Mama says, Harlan,
you get a wish, first night under a new quilt.
It got real quiet, then here he come
running. I'd put out the light,
he knocked his shin on the cedar chest
trying to get to me on the bed.

I was fixing to fold it up, get it
out of my sight, when the siren blowed.
I didn't go. I already knowed.
The quilt was ruint. Big oily smudges
and coal-black handprints where he hadn't

finished washing up. I cried and carried on so
when I seen it that morning
he couldn't look at me before he left,
it made him feel so dirty and bad.

I turned the quilt over on the bed
to keep them on me,
Harlan's hands.

Fortune

We must take our life into our hands,
he said, and his hands bought tickets
for the ship that brought us here, far
from my kitchen full of cousins and aunts,
mother and sisters, to this place
where the women walk wide
past my door. Because of my earrings
they think I know more of what will happen
than they want to know. So I stay
in my kitchen alone, but for the girls
who sometimes come, who tell
their mothers' fear. They like the little rings
in my ears and they want to know
what is in their hands. Gently, gently
I fold their fingers closed, to make them
understand. *Your life,* I tell them, *Yes,*
you keep it in your hands.

Walter and His Mama Talk about Angels

Does everbody have one, even coal operators,
even scabs?
    Everbody.
Did you ever see yours?
    Once I did, when you was being born.
    I seen a man, like made of light
    in the corner of the room. He come over
    by the bed, laid his hand on my forehead
    and he said, Poor baby.
Are they all for people, or do some
have different jobs?
    Maybe they do, like maybe
    there's one to watch on the river,
    and one for possums, one that draws
    them pictures in the stars.
Do they live forever, or do they die?
    I don't believe they die.
Where you figure the ones are
that rolls away the stones?

Journal of Catherine Terry
30 November 1920

The trump of the Last Day
could scarce cast such terror
as the siren. It blew
and the world froze. Children
making their way up the hill to the schoolhouse
suddenly stopped, staring at each other
in some nightmare version of their game
of statues. A woman sweeping her porch,
paralyzed, broom mid-thrash.
Another, arms half-lifted in her reach
to a clothesline, face whipped back
toward the siren's wail.
It lasted only a second, this Pompeii,
the terrible tableau vivant,
then everything fell to the ground, clattered
terrible — lunch pails, washtubs, buckets,
brooms — and the world began to pour,
as in a vortex, toward the drift mouth.
It breathed not smoke, but dust — a roof fall,
the mouth of the mountain clamped shut,
eating its children. The siren, merciless.
Merciless the men who got out
fighting rock to get back in.
The eyes of the women, merciless, watching
that mouth for what it would give back
or keep. Don't look, I thought,
for I had never seen a man die —
and wasn't Eurydice lost
on account of just such looking
down toward the underworld? But

their gaze was the only spell they had
to conjure faces out of that dark; it pulled
like a rope on a well bucket, it was a net
flung out between a black sky and a black sea
drawn back empty and flung again.
There was nothing else to do:
like Orpheus, I looked.

II

Raven Light

Raven Light

I must of slept, for I dreamed the fire boss
torching the gas up under the roof
as he come toward me down the hall.
Then I seen he had wings
and that torch was the flaming sword
turning every way at the gate
of the Garden, and I look again
and I see his face all black
and grinning — I think it was a dream.
I think I'm awake. Oh, Christ.
Christ, don't let me be in Hell.
Oh, Jesus. Jesus, Jesus.

■

I'd loaded my second ton,
drilled for the third. Took a notion
I was hungry. I took off my coat,
laid it down on the ground
to set on, and opened
my dinner bucket. Fresh sausage meat
fried up and sandwiched in biscuits,
a apple pie, half-gallon of cold water
in the bottom well of the bucket.
But she'd packed the pie in the top tin,
biscuits and sausage in the middle —
she always done it the other way around.
That was when I heard
the rush of rats to the drift mouth.

When I first come in the mine
Daddy told me, *Them rats*
can hear a branch crack

up on top of the mountain.
They hear the earth start to give
when the roof's about to fall.
Them rats makes a run for the drift mouth,
you drop what you're doing, son,
you run.

        I got so slow
when I heard them. Out in the hall
I seen dust falling thick
about a hundred yards down the way
toward the mouth, I heard beams
start to creak. Dust begin to blow
back where I was, I heard hollering.
I heard praying. I walked back
the other way, into the dark.

■

When I was a boy, I liked the story of Jonah.
He done right, I thought. If God
meant to send him to a evil place,
why shouldn't he get on a boat
and head the other way? I bet Nineveh
was run by folks like Stone Mountain Coal,
men that jokes about using a dago
for a mine post, that figures it's cheaper
to replace a dead miner than
to replace a dead mule. If a whale
swallowed you, at least it wouldn't be
for meanness, nor for money.

■

I feel I could walk a long way,
though I am far past what I know
of the layout of the mine. I left
my dinner and carbide behind
but a man can live
five days if he ain't hurt, taking in
the water he needs through his skin —

for down here, even the air
is mostly water.

■

Pretend.
Pretend it's just you
closing your eyes and not this
god-awful dark.
You're napping by the creek
with Gertie. She's smiling, doing
that thing with the daisy — *he loves me,*
he loves me not. Loves me not.
But it's Jesus I see, instead of her,
plucking petals off that flower
like a boy pulling wings off a fly.
And him not even looking at me
while he makes up his mind.

■

Don't Daddy always come back? I'd say
to Mama when she begin to slam pots
or drop dishes long about shift end.
She got worse when it got down in the fall
and dark come earlier every day —

Like bad news can't wait to get here,
she'd mutter and moan. Then there he'd be,
stomping coal dust off his boots on the porch,
his face blacked and shiny, like it had soaked
up the dark and give it back alive.
He put me in mind of a raven, those times,
and he was beautiful to my eyes.

But it fretted Mama to see him so.
She'd send us to the back room,
he'd set in the washtub, but no matter
how hard we scrubbed he had
them coon eyes, like he was always
looking out from the dark.

■

Lord, I hope Gertie don't remember
she stacked my dinner bucket wrong.
She'll figure it for bad luck, won't nobody
be able to tell her different.

I ain't afraid in my head — there's a part of me
that's like a kite cut loose, like Noah's raven
that knows it ain't going back —
but when I think on Gertie, my knees buckle,
my whole body's set atremble. Like when
I first come to her and she
let me, oh honey,
and seemed like only my body
knowed what was happening.

■

I wisht I could sleep
my way to it, but some miles back
I woke to black pressed flat,
smothering agin my face, and screaming —
screaming worse'n a woman birthing
a seven-month baby —
I thought, *Painter!*
and I throwed up my arms to try
and push it off, but I hit air
and cold rock and of a sudden
I knowed them screams
was coming from me.

God almighty, Goddamn.

Our Father who art in heaven,
who maketh me to lie beneath the green pastures,
God the Father, who gave his only begotten son,
Goddamn, what a hell
of a thing to do.

■

This passage has give out, too low
to walk through, and I ain't fixing
to crawl. Used to be Indians around here
not too awful long ago, and for a minute
I thought I'd found the back end
of one of their caves and this was not
really happening.

That's how simple it would be,
something that'd open.

There is only setting here, now, like Noah
waiting for the storm to pass. He must of pondered
long and hard on how to start over
in a whole new world, not even knowing
who'd be there, or if there'd be trees. Finding out
what it means to not know nothing.

■

Somewhere over top of me now, up on the bald,
is a giant chestnut tree, you can see it
from everywhere in the valley. Mama says
it was already dead when she was a girl.
When I was nine or so, there come
a thunderstorm so wild, lightning
riv'd it right in half — but it's still standing.
Dead as kindling, half a century at least,
and still there. That's got
to mean something, don't it?

When I read the story of Noah,
it was that chestnut tree I pictured
to be the first thing rising up
out of the lowering waters.
First Bible story I ever read on my own —
else I'd never of knowed about the raven,
for Brother Pentecost spoke only of the dove
and the olive branch. That old riven
tree, not what Noah was looking for,
but the raven would of chose the twisted hands

of that old tree, over Noah's solid ground —
if there is any such thing.

■

The cold aches me. My bones
feel like I been stoned, like that woman
in the Bible. What was that for?

I would have a chair, if there was anything
left for me to have. Not a easy
chair but a rocker — back and forth,
back.

■

I imagined Gertie, then ordinary dark
to be the last thing I'd see.
Down here once I seen a sheet of rock
pocked with skeletons of ferns, they looked
as dancing in the rock as they must
of looked in the wind. Nothing
like that here, only one of them dripping rocks
that cones down from the roof just
to grow back up from the floor.
Like a hourglass, but moving so slow
you can't see it go. It drips and the top
don't lose nothing, just grows longer
while the bottom gets taller. I wonder
how long till they touch,
till there ain't nothing at all
between what's coming and what's gone.
How long?

■

I wisht I had something to write with,
but who could ever read such writing
as I could do in this dark?

■

I don't know why I done it. I don't know
why I done it. Come this way.

What I want is to keep seeing Gertie's face
up in the world. I'd give a arm and a leg —
Jesus, I'm laughing and it ain't even funny,
that's a real arm and leg — to of stayed.

I don't know why I come this way.
If we are made in God's image, I bet God
looks something like Henry Burgess. I bet
he could come down here and set his foot
on this rock, prop one elbow on his knee,
lean forward and rub his chin,
like Henry doing a deal on market day,
and say, *Alright, then, son,*
what'll you give me for it? And I'd be dumb
as a little boy again, not one thing
I could tell him worth my life.

So I guess I'll die. I'm dying right now
and I ain't laughing neither. Twenty
years old and crying into my shirt.
I'm glad Gertie can't see me.
But when he seen God

was really gonna make him die, even *Jesus* cried
and tried to change his mind.

■

I was fifteen when we laid Daddy
in the ground. Uncle Bill and Ted Stanley
and Tom and Woody Hartsell
done for Daddy, though usually the women
washes the body and lays it out. They nailed the lid
on Daddy's box afore me nor Mama either one
got a chance to see him. *It's best*, they told her,
and she let it go. The four of them would set
with Daddy through the night, carry him
up the hill in the morning.
I am aiming to carry Daddy, too, I told Uncle Bill.
He started in, *Now, son....* I stopped him,
I said, *I am aiming to do it.*

Daddy was a big man, and when I hefted
the corner of his box onto my left shoulder
I didn't feel hardly no weight at all but the pine.
Uncle Bill watched me. He set his jaw and looked
straight ahead, so that's what I did. After, them four
was out on the back porch drinking. I went on out,
when I knowed Uncle Bill seen me, I stood
tall as I could. *I reckon I'm a man now,* I told him.
I reckon you are, Nathan, he said.
And we all waited for Woody Hartsell
to speak, for he was the eldest man there.
It was a bad roof fall, he said, twenty,
thirty foot section. Daddy was working

back behind, made a run for it.
When the rocks begun to close in,
he lunged, arms flung forward like diving
for cover. They caught him mid-flight,
crushed everthing below his chest, his head
and shoulders and arms was all they brung out.
Woody reached for the jar, swallowed hard,
Jesus Christ, God Almighty, he swore,
I keep seeing him,
jutting out of the rock
like a baby half-born.

■

Out of the dark of the drift mouth
they'll be men still coming out. In twos
and threes, holding each other up, dragging
brothers and fathers between them. Only
the carbide lamps show, no faces. I am part
of the dark the lights bob through in little clusters,
wavery constellations that fade into ordinary
men in the daylight. I am far under
the roots of the old chestnut, hid
in the raven light, where the rock
of ages has cleft.

III.

Winter ~ Summer

Journal of Catherine Terry
5 December 1920

Robert Davis's father and two brothers
are dead and Nathan Stokes is missing.
When they told Mrs. Davis, she slid down
on herself like melting wax on a candle
then shook off the women who rushed
to hold her. She turned — even the air
around her seemed bruised — walked through
the crowd to the wall of fallen rock
blocking the drift mouth
and pressed her ear against it.
Women came and led her off.
                              A dirty arm
on the other side thrust a dinner bucket
through a small opening the men had made
in the rocks. It was passed, with words,
till it came to Gertie Stokes's hand.
The lost, they tell me, are almost
never found, their bodies left adrift,
comfortless in the unhallowed mountain
like sailors lost in the ocean's deep sift.
She did not speak, only turned the bucket
upside-down — the miners' way to signal
strike. Henry Burgess turned his, the gesture
caught, swept through the crowd, and so
it was decided — the men were going out.

A Reporter from New York Asks Edith Mae Chapman, Age Nine, What Her Daddy Tells Her about the Strike

We ain't to go in the company store, mooning
over peppermint sticks, shaming ourselves like a dog
begging under the table. They cut off our account
but we ain't no-accounts. We ain't to go to school
so's the company teacher can tell us we are.
We ain't going to meeting and bow our heads
for the company preacher, who claims it is the meek
will inherit the coal fields, instead of telling
how the mountains will crumble and rocks
rain down like fire upon the heads
of the operators, like it says in the Bible.
We ain't to talk to no dirtscum scabs
and we ain't to talk to God. My daddy
is very upset with the Lord.

The Gospel According to
Stone Mountain Coal

Stone Mountain Coal came to West Virginia
to bring forth the abundance of these hills, to feed
the railroads and ironworks and steel mills
which are the blood and heart and bones
of our land the way the Lord fed the multitude
from two fishes and five loaves. To feed
our country from the coal fields that had lain
fallow generation after generation, waiting
for such men of faith and vision — faith greater
than a grain of mustard seed, who say
unto these mountains, *Remove*, and they
are removed. Who say unto those who upheave
the natural harmony between owners
and workers — a harmony guaranteed
by contracts signed of their own free will —
what the householder said to his laborers
in the Lord's parable of the vineyard: *Friend,*
I do thee no wrong. Didst thou not agree
with me for a penny? Is it not lawful for me
to do what I will with mine own?

Dear Sister

You always was one to fret, but no,
I don't need money, not for food
nor tobacco nor nothing. We got a crop
of city boys down here from the papers
and we got us a poker game going.
You need any money, I can send you some.

> yr. loving brother,
> Oren Ash

My Dearest Hazel

Well, honey, I had not thought of Annabelle
for years. Was you turning seven, or eight,
when Momma made her? I remember Momma
traipsing all the way over to Delsey Salyer's
to trade a bit of green thread for blue
so's Annabelle's eyes'd be same as yours.
And we unravelled Daddy's yellow neck scarf
Momma had knit him 'fore they was married
to make her hair. Hazel, honey, how I remember it is,
she got left under the porch one night that spring
it rained so bad and brung all them mudslides
and copperheads down the hill. Daddy forbid us
to go in under there looking for her. We pried up
a loose board on the porch, got her with Daddy's
fishing pole, but she was ruint, soaked through with mud.
Listen, Hazel, what I remember is, it was me
left Annabelle under the porch. You hear me, honey?
Wasn't nothing you could of done.

Dear Diary

Daddy has scolded me for listening
to him and Uncle Ted, for there is things,
he told me, little girls aint meant
to understand. Nor go around repeating —
and here is where he ducked his chin
and looked at me out from under his
eyebrows, so I'd know not to tell
how they are waiting for the dogwood
to bloom in spring, so they can hide
in the flowers and greening, and pick
off scabs, shooting down the hillside.
A man, Daddy says, has got to make a stand
and say what side he's on. *And we aint*
on the side of no scabs, are we Edith Mae?
No, Daddy, we aint, I told him true.
But I will tell you, Dear Diary, I believe
them dogwoods been hurt enough — being used
for the cross, and now for this. Them trees
aint asked to be on nobody's side.
And I am on the side of the trees.

Ash Wednesday

We do not speak of home, her mother
and sisters, the river, the Church.
There is no priest here, we go
unconfessed, save the sign and words
we say for each other in the mornings
when I go to my shift — *Ego te absolvo.*
God will know. They murder our Nico
and still she makes for me the sign,
the words. Now we enter *la Quaresima,*
tempo di penitenza, e ceneri.
I put my finger in the cold ash
of the stove, make on her forehead
the sign of the cross. She makes
for me the sign, but my face,
it is so gray from the coal dust
that it does not show, the cross,
la penitenza, la culpa, quantissimo,
Valentina, tutto lo lamento.

Sang

After Harlan, I don't hardly remember.
Like the brain fever when I was five —
I come out the other side not able to walk
nor talk nor, Mama says, even cry.
Mama and Daddy brung me home.
I told Mama, I said, *I can't bear it.*
No, you can't, Ina, she said. *But you will.*
And she give me a basket to go hunt sang
up on the hill. There's hardly any left
with perfect roots — they'll be missing both arms
or a leg below the knee or a piece of the face.
You can't find a whole man. Still,
the work feels good to my hands — digging
down into the dirt, pulling out the little men.

Another Book Report, by Pearlie Webb

I did not mean to start nothing with that other book report, Miss Terry. I am glad you like my *thoughts,* as you say, Miss Terry, but do not figure I go around thinking all the time. I got work to do for Mama. But when I told her the story of Orpheus and Eurydice and how you said to compare it to something *in my own experience,* Mama got a funny look on her face — she has been queer since the siren — and she has said, *Sit down, Pearlie, and do it.*

This story reminds me of "The Farmer's Curst Wife," which is a old song my Mamaw Webb used to sing. This song will also make you think of Persephone, for the Devil comes up out of the ground to take somebody back down with him. Now, this farmer wants the Devil to take his wife, which is like Lot again, only this song makes out like it's funny. So the Devil, he takes her down to Hell, and this is like Eurydice, who is also a wife and also gets took down to Hell. Now, from these two stories, I see two ways for a woman to get out of Hell. In the *Changes* book way, the husband begs and they tell him he can have her back, but he's got to not look at her all the way home. In my own experience, this is a bad thing to tell a man, for you can't hardly keep a man from looking. This ain't much of a deal for her, is what I say.

In Mamaw's song, when the farmer's wife gets down to Hell she starts beating up them little devils, splitting out their brains with a hatchet and such as that, till one of them says *Take her back, Daddy, she's a-murdering us all.* She gets herself out, and when she gets home she paddles her old man in the head with a butterstick for sending her down there in the first place. This is very different from Eurydice who just *dies a second death* and *did not reproach her husband,* as it says in the *Changes* book. I think Eurydice needed her a butterstick, I told Mama, and she laughed — but I was not meaning to be funny.

I conclude that it is better to be curst by a husband like the farmer in Mamaw's song than it is to be loved by a husband like Orpheus. It seems like if you are a wife you are going to Hell no matter what, but at least in Mamaw's song —

There's one advantage women have over men.
A woman can go to Hell and come back again.

My Dearest Hazel

I am so lonesome for you, Hazel,
for you and Momma, that some days
I think I will die of it. But, honey,
do not come down here. Do you hear me,
Hazel? Do not. The guards are not letting
anybody in nor out of the camp anyway.
Probably you don't know, being
up there to Momma's — Sid Hatfield
and Mayor Testerman, down to Matewan,
has killed seven Baldwin-Felts
in a shootout, including two brothers
of Thomas Felts of Bluefield.
Three of our boys is also dead,
the Mayor is one. It is a bad mean
time down here, Hazel. The newspapers
is calling us "Bloody Mingo County,"
and it is for true. Clayton, he ain't
had no dealings with the union,
but last night he was walking by the river
with some other men in the dark,
and a passel of them Baldwin-Felts,
all loaded up with shotguns in the back
of a truck, come looking for this man
that was walking with the others.
He ducked behind Clayton to hide
— that guard couldn't see no faces
in the dark, and he stuck the end of his
gun barrel right between Clayton's eyes.
Next morning that guard was on the old
rope footbridge over Little Tug Creek,
and somebody waiting on the other side

shot him three times in the chest.
This is what is happening down here, Hazel,
it is trouble and then some. We are all
in it now, like it or not. This whole camp
is like a mine with a hollow-sounding roof,
and hid up there in the mountain above us,
where we can't see it and can't nothing
hold it up, that old kettle bottom
is waiting to drop.

Lick Creek Tent Colony

Whoever it was took a shot at Don Chafin
needs took up the hill and the tar beat out of him.
I don't care if Don Chafin is Satan walking
the earth, he is the sheriff and you can't shoot
at the law and not bring them down on your head.
We got babies down here. We ain't got no houses,
but we got babies. When this union business
started up, first thing the Company did
was turn us out — chester drawers and marriage
beds and womenfolk in the family way
standing out in the road. Men promised
it'd be over by spring. Now here we are,
union tents the only thing keeping
evening damp off these babies' faces.
Last night Baldwin-Felts and sheriff's deputies
rode through, shooting in the air and slashing
tents with bayonets, so now we ain't even got that.
Them fool men got theirselves so riled
they can't think of nothing but bringing
Don Chafin's head home on a platter.
They ought to turn around and take a good look
at the morning after — babies' heads everywhere,
popping up through the holes in the tents.

What History Means to Me

ROBERT DAVIS, *Grade 4*

History is the story of what has happened, like when Papaw
Clyde tells about Mother Jones in '02. It is also now, like
when Baldwin-Felts knocks on folks door to put them out
when their Daddy joins the union or gets killed in the mine,
and says, *Your history.*

EDITH MAE CHAPMAN, *Grade 4*

I aint to do this assignment, Daddy says, even if it means
I cant come back to school which I hope it dont, for when
we was farming I could not come many days and now that
we are at Winco Mama and Daddy has said *go ahead and
go.* But now Daddy has got all mad and stomping around
which makes you wish you was somewhere else and makes
Mama say *Now John,* for Daddy is also swearing and he
says I must write this down exactly and not one word more
— *There aint no company teacher got nothing to teach us
children about history.*

WALTER COYLE, *Grade 5*

Me and Uncle Joe loves snow cream better than God,
Mama says. We'd go out no matter how bitter cold, get us
a bucketful of snow, so clean and white. Mama'd stir in the
sugar and cream and we'd eat till it come out our ears. Uncle
Joe is dead now, at Layland, and there ain't no more snow
cream, for the coal dust settles on the snow afore you can
get to it, and Mama says I got better things than that to cry
about.

GLADDIE BEECHAM, *Grade 6*

I have asked Aunt Mandy Beecham, for she is the oldest
person alive that I know, she remembers from before the

War, before we was West Virginia and was only the Endless Mountains of Virginia. She has put it to me like this. First the railroads come and lots of fancy pants forriners trying to buy up ever little creek and holler and home place they set their thieving eyes on. Then the timber men come, took the oak and yellow poplar, wrecked the rivers and left. Collieries come and stayed, but the coal and the money went. What it means to us is a lot of dead husbands and caved-in bellies, and a whole crop of outlander missionaries and bankers figuring they got to come down here and take and raise us.

PEARLIE WEBB, *Grade 8*
History is the facts, and true, whereas stories is what folks make up, is what Miss Madden taught us last year. Well, just last month, Ory Price died trying to have a baby. She lived in the house next to ours, I heard it all, it was the awfullest thing. This was a week or so after Matewan, it was Marshall Law and the Baldwin-Felts wouldn't let nobody in nor out of the camp. Not even the granny woman come to help Ory, though they must of could hear her screaming for Jesus all the way down to the road. Woman come down from Colored row to try and help, but it was too late. Company doctor showed up after it got quiet. My daddy had took Ray Price up the hill, whilst Mama and Aunt Elsie washed Ory and cleaned up the back room. Doctor come to write up the Death Certificate, for Cause of Death he put *Childbirth,* which is a fact, Miss Terry, but it sure ain't got nothing to do with the truth.

Dear Sister

Do not believe what all you read
in the papers, Leona, about the strikers
being reds. It is true, the Communist Party
of New York sent down a truckload
of potatoes. You will find them rotted
where our boys turned that truck over
down by the creek bottom. Not a one took.
We got people down here that's hungry
but *not* for *Communist* potatoes.

                                yr. loving brother,
                                Oren Ash

Dear Mr. President
Blair Mountain, West Virginia

You do not know me,
although according to Sargent Platt
you were my commander-in-chief when I served
in France, 1916 to 1917.
I was not but 19 when I went to the Great War,
but when Sargent Platt said *Stand your ground, men,*
I stood it. Even when the planes come, with gas,
and I seen them without masks melt down
from the inside, screaming, like their lungs
was a spider web lit on fire.

Then I come back here, to West Virginia,
to the coal mines. I have seen a whole trip car
of men drug by a mule through a pocket of black damp,
which is carbon dioxide, if you don't know, the men
all lop-headed and limp-armed,
same trickle of blood out the corner
of their mouth as them boys in France.

Now I look up out of my tent, which Al Burgess
has let us strikers set on his place, and again
I see planes, of the United States of America,
waiting for your order to drop their gas
on the coal miners of West Virginia.
A lot of us down here has been to the War,
and all of us has been in the mines.
You can kill us, Mr. President,
we all know that. But what in the world
makes you think you can scare us?

A Reporter from Boston Comes to Lick Creek

He come in here, same grabby look on his face
as them that come through buying up mineral rights.
Doing some big job for some big boss. Got to find out
what you got, and get it out of you. I told him
straight out, *We got three babies — two and four
and five year old — and this cookpot and this tent
and the clothes on our back. First frost right around
the bend and no end in sight. It's a good thing,*
he says, *you got the union behind you.* He says,
Would you care to say a few words about that?
Oh, I'll give you a few words for that, I told him,
but he cut me off. Says his boss's wife has heard
how we got some *beautiful ballads* down here
and would I sing him one, so he can tell her
about it. Can you believe that?
I wanted to snatch that man bald-headed —
but then I thought better of it. *Sure,* I said,
I got one for you, starts like this —

> *I'll tell you all a story about Omie Wise,*
> *And how she was deluded by John Lewis's lies.*

Henry Burgess Decides to Go Back In

It don't do to think too much about it.
The others is all going back in.
First you got to eat, then you can think
about thinking. Deal with the gun
that's aimed at you, is what I say.
Things got set up this way
way back before we was ever born.
Whoever's great-grandaddy first swindled
somebody else's great-grandaddy
out of his land and his life —
may he rot in Hell.
At least we picked up our guns.
At least for a while we could walk upright.
I told Mary, *Now don't you tell
nobody else,* when she told me
what Gertie Stokes told her.
How she didn't aim to start nothing
with that dinner bucket. It was only
when they give it to her, she seen
she'd stacked it wrong and her being
in such a state — trying to take it in
that Nathan was killed — she just
turned it over, trying to turn the bad luck
the way you'd reach out quick to right a pitcher
knocked over on the table, for its own sake,
even after the milk is spilled.

One Voice

And he came into all the country about Jordan,
preaching the baptism of repentance for the remission
of sins.... The voice of one crying in the wilderness,
Prepare ye the way of the Lord, make his paths straight.
                                        — Luke 3:4–5

Brothers and sisters, I have blasphemed
in your eyes. I have heard the talk and seen
your faces turn away. It is true —
I baptized a sinner in Tug River
in the name of the Father, of the Son,
and of John L. Lewis. Did not John the Baptist
say unto the people, *Let him who hath two coats*
impart unto him that hath none? Any operators
stop you on your way to church this morning
and impart? Any of you leave a child
at home, on account of it wasn't their turn
with the coat? Did not John
say unto the publicans, *Exact no more*
than that which is appointed you? Yet who
among you has not broke body and soul
loading six ton of coal day-in and day-out,
and been told that you owe?
Do you not hear in the words of John
the voice of the union crying in the wilderness?
Oh, my brothers and sisters, wait not, Jesus
himself has said it, *Whatsoever ye bind*
on earth shall be bound in heaven,
and what ye loose on earth shall be loosed
in heaven. We are *here,* in Williamson,
West Virginia, brothers and sisters, look not

for the heavens to open for we are, in the words
of Zacharias the prophet, *them that sit
in darkness.* Look not for the wings of the dove
to guide you, a creature of light, she is blind
in the unquenchable night of the hole. Look
to the raven, for she is of our world, and oh
my brothers and oh my sisters, only the darkness
can teach us to walk through the dark.

Sheepskin

I told that doctor flat out
what it was. He looks me right
in my face, says, *Mrs. Chapman,*
you can worry a man sick, now,
and John has got to work.
You let me do the doctoring here,
unless you got a sheepskin
somewhere I don't know about.

All I could think was that old
story about a wolf in sheep's
clothing. I said, *Sheepskin?*
And he points to a picture frame
propped on his desk, diploma
wrote in Latin, from some college
in Virginia. I said, *No, doctor,*
I got nothing like that.

I did not hold John's hands,
speckled with coal tattoos,
out to the doctor, did not say
Read this here, doctor, how easy
the dust works in under his skin.
I did not say, You come home
with us. Read his handkerchiefs,
read my pillowslips, grayed
with dust, sprayed with coal-black
flecks of coughed-up muck. I did
not tell him my learning come nights,
from the ragged, rocky-chested racket
of my daddy's cough and the only

Latin we got to show for it
is on his stone.

No. *What I know is not wrote*
on sheepskin, doctor, I told him.
I said, *What I know*
is wrote on the wall.

Samson

Pillars is the walls of coal you leave
between rooms while you working
the rooms — Boss had me explain it
to the Big Boss come down from Boston
on the train to lay eyes on things.
Boss didn't call me by my name,

just holler, *Come on over here, son.*
Bragged how big I is, how strong
a colored boy get when he shovel and haul.
Didn't ask me how my eye got gone —
coal shot out when I was pillar-drawing.
Didn't ask my name, neither one.

I played along. *Yessir,* I told them,
them pillars is coal, they can get sold.
We come back in when the rooms is all mined
and pull them down, we don't leave nothing
behind. I've knowed three men's died that way,
nothing left of them but their names —

roof don't hold too long without no walls.
Bosses begin to edge back toward the hall.
I stood in their way. With my right hand
I pressed one pillar, the other with my left.
I explained — *To the mountain we all the same.*
I pressed harder, and I told them my name.

Milk

Mama always said, You can't feed a baby
if there's no happiness in the milk. Now, we
didn't judge a man by what he had, but
by whether he took his pay home
before he went to the bar, and Burns Cantrell
did not. And he hit Meardie, which wasn't
no fault of hers, Mama said. So when she
had a baby come in strike time, Mama
bought two tins of canned milk out of
the dollar a week the company store
allowed each family for food, and sent me
to set them on Cantrells' porch every Monday
after Burns had went up the hill. Now,
it was the law among the miners that, come
a roof fall, you run. Everybody knowed
that was how it was. If you stop and look back
to see who's dead or trapped, you
only make more dead. Four days after the men
went back in, there come a bad roof fall, killed
sixteen. Daddy was back behind. Right off
the rocks broke one backbone and his jaw
in five places. Burns Cantrell was up front.
He heard them rocks begin to fall, and he run
back into the hole, pitch black, the mountain
crumbling like the end of the world,
and carried Daddy out. He knowed
he owed my mama for the milk.

Good Man in the Mine

That what they say.
It like a badge,
make you white
in the mine. Make you
a good man —
in the mine.

Oh, boss still start you
where the seam
be all wet and low.
Till somebody see
ain't nobody dying
round where you go.

Then the white miners
finally decides
if you be a good
man in the mine.
They gives the word —
nobody dying.

We *all* colored
down there in the dirt
and the dark. It alright,
long as we ain't out
in the light. It alright,
if it save their life.

David

At home, in Carrara, Papa he is *mastro
di tagliapietra*, master stonecutter, maker
of beautiful buildings and bridges. Rich men
they knock on our door, asking *licenza*
to enter our house, to talk with Papa
about a portico, or a piazza.
Papa he loves the stone.
He takes me to see the David, for what
is Michelangelo, he tells me, if not a stonecutter.
La differenza, he says, is that when Papa
sees a stone he sees inside it the face
of a beautiful building. Michelangelo
he sees a beautiful man.
Then he cuts away from the stone
everything that is not David.

Papa wants to come here because America
is a land of beautiful buildings still
hiding in their stones. He believes
he can uncover those buildings,
scoprire la belleza nascosta nella pietra.
When we arrive, he tells the men
with the books — *roccia, pietra* — and he makes
the motion of hitting the stone. They point
to a train. When the train stops, they give Papa
not a chisel, but a shovel. He shakes his head, *no,
no, no* — but already we owe for the train.

Papa tries to pay, he goes every day
into the mountain, into the stone. It seals
him in. *Sealed in*, the men from the company

they tell Mamma the roof it fell, they are sorry.
No survivors, too dangerous to try to bring
the bodies out. The rich men here, they see nothing
in the stone but money. *Non c'e nessuno che vede*
il mio papa e gli altri nella pietra. No Michelangelo
here to cut the stone away from the beautiful men.

Woody Hartsell Tells about Walter's First Day

Now there's some that says that boy ain't right,
and you might of been among them, had you seen
Walter throwed over Tom Coyle's shoulder,
Tom a-running for the drift mouth and Walter
a-twisting and shrieking *My legs, Daddy,*
Daddy, my legs!
                  Jesus Christ, God Almighty,
stopped your heart to hear it. We run after them,
turned out Tom had blasted and Walter
had looked down and not seen nothing below his belt
but dust. Figured the dynamite had blowed his legs
clean away. Screaming worse'n a painter, worse'n
bloody murder, screaming *I'm kilt, Daddy!*
Daddy, it's a-trying to kill me!
                  Poor baby,
he's right as rain.

The Mother Has Her Say

I have heard of a land, on a faraway strand,
It's a beautiful home of the soul,
Built by Jesus on high, where we never shall die,
It's a land where we never grow old.

Let Odell bury the boy hisself, is what I say.
I said it to his face, *I bore him myself,*
you do the burying. I told him, I *told* him,
don't matter Danny's big and tall for thirteen,
he got the sense of a boy, not a man. Odell swore
the boy'd not go in, just stand at the belt
and pick slate out of the coal, and I told him,
I said, *What are you talking to me for?*
You done made up your mind. You ain't come
to ask my yea or nay. Them boys, they don't
see nothing, nor smell nothing, they think
ain't nothing there. I know they warned him
about that pocket of black damp
and he figured to take the shortcut anyway,
go in, surprise his daddy. Figured
to hold his breath. Sweet
Jesus God.

Mama come, and tried to shame me
into going to the church, and I told her,
I ain't going to do it, Mama. Don't need
to go sing about some faraway home.
Ain't I already living in a land
where a boy can't never grow old?

Notes

The epigraph comes from the poem "Gauley Bridge" in Muriel Rukeyser's *U.S. 1: The Book of the Dead*. This book tells the story of the deaths of over a thousand people, mostly black workers, from silicosis after tunneling through Gauley Mountain, West Virginia, in order to divert the New River for a hydroelectric plant for Union Carbide.

"L'Inglese": The last two lines of "L'Inglese" repeat the motto over the entrance to Dante's Inferno: Leave behind all hope, Ye who enter here.

"Jake and Isom": Yellow-dog contracts were those in which miners agreed as a condition of their employment not to belong to any labor union.

"The Dancers Are All Gone under the Hill": The title of this poem comes from "East Coker" by T. S. Eliot, and its last line comes from Ecclesiastes.

"Raven Light": *Painter* is a mountain word for the panther, or bobcat.

"Sang": *Sang* is a mountain word for ginseng.

"A Reporter from Boston Comes to Lick Creek": "Little Omie Wise" is one of a number of mountain songs which tell the story of a young girl lured into sex by a promise of marriage and then murdered by the young man. John Lewis is the name of the man who murders little Omie.

"The Mother Has Her Say": The epigraph to this poem comes from an old hymn, "The Land Where We Never Grow Old."

The "Dear Sister" poems and "Milk" are dedicated to Leona Mello, who gave me the stories, and to her mother, Marie Ash, who gave the milk.

The "My Dearest Hazel" poems are dedicated to Eleanor Wilner.

About the Author

Diane Gilliam Fisher was born and grew up in Columbus, Ohio. Her family was part of the Appalachian outmigration from Mingo County, West Virginia, and Johnson County, Kentucky. Fisher has a PhD in Romance Languages and Literature from Ohio State University and an MFA from the Warren Wilson Program for Writers. In 2003, she received an Individual Artist Fellowship from the Ohio Arts Council, and her first book, *One of Everything,* was published by Cleveland State University Poetry Center. Her chapbook, *Recipe for Blackberry Cake,* was published by Kent State University Press in 1999. Fisher lives in Brimfield, Ohio, with her husband and two daughters.